Table Of Contents

CHAPTER 1

WHAT IS DOMESTIC VIOLENCE?

Domestic violence or domestic abuse is when a loved one or intimate partner deliberately causes harm to the significant other. It could be the husband hurting his wife which is the most common form of domestic violence or it could be the wife hurting her husband or parents harming children and vice versa, also it could be siblings harming another sibling. It could also be an ex-wife or ex-husband or ex-boyfriend coming back to hurt the former partner

Most of the Cases are Men who abuse their wives or girlfriends.

Domestic abuse is always misdiagnosed it is different from regular marital conflict. It is Solely caused by the abuser the victim cannot fix it or control it she can only leave the abuser.

DEFEAT DOMESTIC VIOLENCE

Read This Before You Get Into A Relationship

Let's put an end to femicide
Escape before you are killed

The partner I'm living with is not the person I fell in love with. Beat Domestic violence handbook

By:

BEBUH DIVINE

An abuser is like poison the only solution to poison is to leave it. If you keep consuming it will keep harming you.

Abuse it not Gods fault it is your fault you made the wrong choice ignored red flags and married an abuser

What do you do when you miss the road you don't blame God you simply put the GPS pay attention to road signs and get to the right road

It is the same with marriage and relationship. If you ignore red flags of abuse and make a wrong choice you will have to face reality. plan carefully and leave the relationship.

When bend iron over and over it breaks that's what a narcissist or abuser is doing with you may be in denial but your body will tell you when start having health problems due to abuse you know you are not just enduring an abuser but you are slowly committing suicide.

The Cycle of Domestic Abuse

Domestic abuse usually occurs in a circle. The abuser will put the victim on a pedestal with sweet love bombing then radically changes suddenly and abuse the victim, then apologises and promises it won't happen then blames the victim and the victim will be waiting for the good moments of praise creating a toxic bond which is a circle that never ends until the death of a partner or the victim leaves to a safe place

The Graph of Domestic Violence

A normal relationship is like a boat ride it is smooth most of the time there may be a few bumps or storms here and there it is ok no one is perfect but a domestic abuse relationship is a like a rollercoaster up down up down which will end up wearing and rearing the victim you will end up with sicknesses like depression, arthritis **STD´S PTSD OR DEATH.**

DOMESTIC ABUSE GRAPH

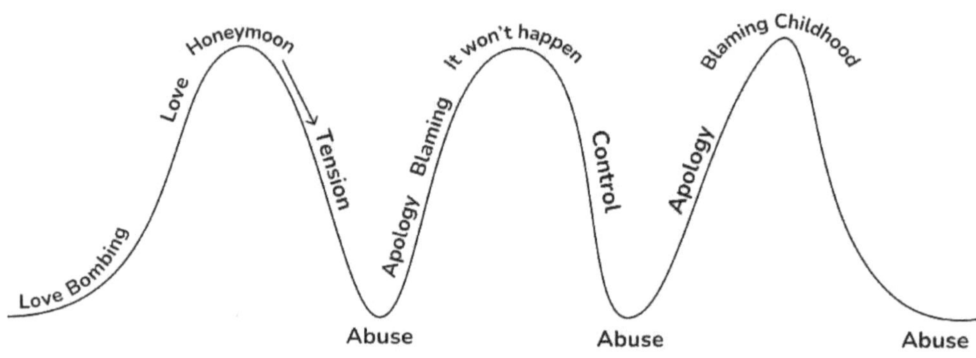

Alarming Statistics of Domestic Violence

People from all social status can suffer or have suffered from domestic abuse. Presidents, millionaires, first ladies, most women from all works of life and social status have either personally suffered domestic violence or know someone who has suffered domestic violence Domestic violence has no respect for race, class, wealth, power position or gender. It is rampant and everywhere.

2300 women are killed every year in Europe at the hands of their partners or ex-partners. **45 women a week** are killed by those who supposedly loved them. 1 in 3 women have suffered physical and/or sexual violence and 1 in 2 women have experienced sexual harassment since the **age of 15**.

According to the National Family Health Survey (NFHS), 2019-2021, "29.3 per cent of married Indian women between the ages of 18 and 49 have experienced domestic/sexual violence; 3.1 per cent of pregnant women aged 18 to 49 have suffered physical violence during their pregnancy."

Nearly 20 people per minute in the USA are abused by their intimate partner which adds up to 10 million people a year

As I write this book a Ugandan athlete Rebecca Cheptegei was killed by her husband who poured petrol on her and burnt her to death this is horrible

I remember gospel artist Osinachi Nwachukwu killed by her husband. I also remember Gabbi Petito killed by her fiance. The list is endless. I am sick and tired of seeing beautiful people getting killed by monsters.

God's Opinion About Domestic Violence

God was so angry about violence in the days of Noah that he regretted that he created the world so God hates violence vehemently

Genesis 6 :11-13

11 Now the earth was corrupt in God's sight and was full of violence. 12 God saw how corrupt the earth had become, for all the people on earth had corrupted their ways. 13 So
God said to Noah, "I am going to put an end to all people, for the earth is

Proverbs 3:31

31 Do not envy the violent or choose any of their ways.

Psalms 11:5

5 The LORD examines the righteous, but the wicked, those who love violence, he hates with a passion.

- **It is not God plan for you to live in abuse fear isolation tension oppression, brutality**
- **It is the plan of the devil to kill steal and destroy.**
- **It is God's plan for you to have life and have it in abondance**
- **If you are being abused it is Not Gods plan for you it is time for you to leave**

Chapter 2

WARNING SIGNS OF AN ABUSER

An Abuser Will Have Either One Or More of These Characteristics

1. **ISOLATION:** Abusers usually don't want you to visit or communicate with friends and family. Abusers will create a rift between you and your friends and family. Most will make you choose between them and your family or move you to a place where you are distant from friends and family
2. **UNPREDICTABLE CHARACTER:** Disappears without explanation and leaves you wondering where he is
3. **CONTROLLING BEHAVIOUR:** Tells you what to wear how to shave, where to go whom to be friends with etc
4. **INSULTS YOUR PARENTS:** Never keep a relationship where a partner is abusing your parents it's the worst red flag

5. **ABANDONS YOU AND LEAVES IN A PLACE:** Abusers a good at leaving you in a place stranded

6. **VERY NICE AND SWEET AT FIRST:** Initially they are very kind and sweet to lure you in. But they will drastically change once you move in. They are so nice on purpose so as to keep you in the cycle of abuse then you will be graving for the nice moments

7. **QUICK LOVE:** Beware if your relationship develops too quickly.

8. **FEAR:** If a man instils fear in you, he is preparing you for abuse.

9. **MAKING EXCUSES FOR THE ABUSERS CHARACTER:** Once you are making excuses for the bad character of a partner you are being abused.

10. **LOVE BOMBING AT THE BEGINNING:** An abuser will put you on a pedestal initially then drastically changes and abuses so that you keep longing for the love bombing period

11. **BODY SHAMING:** Example is I like slimmer women, or 75kg is the best weight for you or you are fat this are signs of abuse

12. **TREATS:** In general, are a red flag. Any object can be used to threaten you a knife a gun etc

13. **HARM:** Threatening to harm you and or your loved ones or your pet is a sign of abuse

14. **MANIPULATIVE CHARACTER ABUSERS:** Are very manipulative

15. **INFLICTING PAIN ON YOU ABUSERS:** Derive joy when you are in pain. so, they will inflict pain on you to feed their dark passion they will burn you push shove throw objects

16. **EVIL JOKES:** Jokingly hitting pinching hurting you. Shoving you are red flags you must not miss the more you tolerate the more they escalate

17. **DEPENCY:** Making you super dependent on them for food water money freedom sleep are all tactics of control abusers use to keep you enslaved

18. **OBEDIENCE AGREEMENT:** some abusers go as far as making you sign an obedience agreement. These are all tactics to control and subdue you. If you are in a relationship and you are not meeting or calling friends and family it's a bad sign you are in an abusive relationship

19. **BLAMING YOU FOR BEING ABUSED:** Telling you it is your fault why they abuse you. Example if you stayed in the room, I will not have

bitten you or Blaming alcohol or childhood trauma is the tactics used by abusers to explain their abuse

20. **ACTING** Abusers are the best actors and the most apologetic people in the world
21. **GASLIGHTING** is a sign of abuse (denying your reality) is all about making you feel you have memory problems so that you start doubting your mental ability. When you feel you need to record the discussions with your partner, he is gaslighting you.
22. **THREATENING TO HARM HIMSELF** if you don't do something. It is a very effective tool they use to keep you in line
23. **SUDDEN MODE CHANGES(SNAPS)** Abusers have two or three personalities. They can suddenly change to a monster in seconds and suddenly go back to normal
24. **MAKES YOU FEEL YOU ARE WORTHLESS** abusers will call you slot, beach, hore, fat, pig, slave, dog, etc are all ways used by abusers to erode your self-esteem so that they can keep controlling and abusing you.
25. **WORKING SO HARD TO PLEASE AN ABUSER** If you are working so hard to prove you are good enough for him you are being abused
26. **NEVER APPRECIATE YOUR EFFORTS** Abusers don't appreciate your efforts because you are as good at death is their eyes
27. **PUSHING AND SHOVING** Pushing you and shoving you out of the way is a huge red flag
28. **HITTING YOU AND LAUGHING** This is a red flag you must not ignore
29. **SHOOTING THINGS OR OBJECTS** at you this is a good sign you are dealing with a monster
30. **ABUSERS ARE CLEVER DEVILS** They put you on a pedestal then once you are fully lured into their web, then abuse begins.
31. **PUNCHING THE WALLS** This is a huge red flag of worse things to come
32. **PUSHING YOU DOWN THE STAIRS** It is one of the dark fantasies of abusers enjoy doing
33. **TORTURE.** An abuser seeks to torture you psychologically emotionally, financial, sexually and physically is he has the opportunity once they are done with you are either dead or have PTSD so beware.
34. Once you are making excuses for a man's bad behaviour you are being abused.

35. **TENSION** Feeling tense always when your partner is around is a sign that you are being abused

36. **LIVING ON EGG SHELLS**, i.e. Being so careful with what you say or do to your partner.

37. **FEELING WORTHLESS** If you feel worthless in a relationship it is an abusive relationship

38. If you feel invisible it's a red flag

39. If your opinion doesn't matter it's a red flag

40. If you are constantly being disrespected you are being abused.

41. **BELITTLING** If He Insults you and belittles you it is a huge red flag

42. Temper tantrums especially when you don't obey them is a sign you must not ignore

43. **FALSE ACCUSATIONS** of cheating with no basis are good tactics in abuser's playbook of manipulation

44. **MAKING YOU FEEL UNSAFE** If you feel unsafe in a relationship you are being abused.

45. **POSSESSIVE CONTROL.** The abuser sees you as his possession. If your intimate partner controls what you wear or where you go, he is abusing you

46. **POSING AS THE MOST IMPORTANT PERSON IN YOUR LIFE** a person who poses as the most important and makes all the rules while you the victim follow the rules is an abuser

47. **LIMITING YOUR ACCESS TO MONEY** is a huge red flag

48. **OVERLY JEALOUS** is a huge red flag abusers don't want you around anyone else including your parents you may think it's love and attention in the beginning but it will escalate

49. **MONITORING:** Abusers usually monitor your phone and track your car if you are being washed 24/7, you are effectively a prisoner, and you could be at risk if you don't carefully plan an exit.

50. **ACTING REMORSEFUL:** Abusers are the best actors and the most apologetic people in the world. They may call you 50 to 100 times a day to beg and put you on a pedestal, just for you to come back. But once you're in, you'll pay for their begging 10 times over/

51. **BREAKS YOUR SELF-CONFIDENCE:** Abusers are good at eroding your self-confidence the more you stay with them the more they reduce you to a slave.

52. **DRUG ADDICTS OR TAKING DRUGS:** Many studies have shown that 98 % of drug users or addicts are abusers.

53. **EVIL WRITINGS:** This is a huge red flag. A person who enjoys writing stories about a woman killed and thrown in the forest is a red flag. A good example is the murderer of Lueck Mackenzie June 17 2019 A.A. he loved to write about killing women in a violent manner.
54. **TOO MUCH PHONE CALLING:** Abusers become desperate when you try to leave so they will call you 100 times a day send 50 emails until to lure you back in if you return you will pay dearly for trying to leave in the first place.
55. **STALKING:** Stocking is the worst sign of abuser if a person is stalking you your life is in severe danger move to another state or change your phone number suspend your social media presence vanish for a while at least 6 months to a year.
56. **PREVENTION:** Prevents you from going to the hospital eating or sleeping.
57. **PRESSURE ABUSERS:** Typically put pressure on you to have sex when you don't want to or to perform sexual acts you are not comfortable with.
58. **PRESSURES YOU TO DO DRUGS OR ALCOHOL:** Abusers who do drugs will typically pressure to do drugs with them and drink alcohol with them.
59. **YELLING:** Yelling is a tactic abusers use to tell you are beneath them it is a reg flag.
60. **CRUELTY:** to you your children or to your animals is a huge red flag
61. **HOLDING YOU HOSTAGE:** Some Abusers also hold their victim's hostage depriving them of food water health care.
62. **DISRESPECT:** Someone who has no respect for you or your family, especially parents is a bad sign.
63. **NO REGARD FOR YOUR OPINION:** Someone who has no regard for your opinion is an abuser.
64. **LACK OF EMPATHY:** An abuser does not feel pity for the victim or other abusers don't feel for anyone else but themselves.
65. **CHRONICALLY ENTITLED:** Most abusers have the character of severe entitlement it is a red flag.
66. **ARROGANCE:** arrogance is the typical characteristic of an abuser beware.
67. **CONDESCENDENCE:** Looking down on the victim is their nature you will always be beneath them.

68. **EXPLOITATIVE:** All abusers exploit not only their victims but attempt to exploit people they deal with on a daily basis.
69. **CONTEMPTUOUS:** When the abuser wants to abuse you, you can see the contempt in their face.
70. **DECEPTIVE:** Most abusers usually deceive their victims many times and not only their victims but try to deceive the world by appearing nice in public while they are monstrous in private.
71. **NEVER TAKE RESPONSIBILITY:** They always blame the victim, or alcohol or drugs or their past it is never their fault.
72. **CANNOT TAKE CRITICISM:** If you attempt to criticise an abuser, he will get angry an abuse you the more.

CHAPTER 3

SIGNS SOMEONE IS SUFFERING FROM ABUSE

Defending The Abuser

This is due to the controlling fear instilled in them by the abuser. If they don't say what will keep the abuser out of trouble, once the police or people leave, he will abuse them double. Victims will say I did it to myself or I hit him first

Isolation

If your friend or relative suddenly becomes distant and difficult to visit or contact after getting into a relationship, she is probably being abused.

- Scratch marks
- Dark eyes
- Unexplained bruises wounds
- Dressing odd for the weather to cover injuries
- Playing down abuse
- Hair loss or unusual hair damage
- Loss of financial control
- Unexplained injuries
- Difficulty to contact the person
- Always indoors
- Neck marks of choking
- Missing tooth
- Swollen face or body part.
- Low self esteem
- Scared if you are scared of your partner, you are being abused
- Depression
- Never having money
- Absent without a valid excuse from job school or social engagements.
- Afraid of their partner
- Change of character
- Very quiet.

Chapter 4

Various Kinds Of Domestic Abuse

Verbal Abuse and Psychological

An abuser usually uses derogatory words to destroy you and erode you they will usually call you names like. Beach, stupid, fat, slot, dog, hore

- Embarrassing you before friends,
- Blaming you for all bad things that happen,
- Blaming you for being abused,
- Bringing your moral and self-esteem down,
- Telling you how ugly you dress or look,
- Sees nothing good in you.
- If a partner always insults you, you are in an abusive relationship the insult of abusers is usually very derogatory, slot, beach, fat, hore, prostitute etc

Financial Deprivation and Control

- Telling you how terrible you are or how bad you dress.

Financial Deprivation and Control

- Controls all the money and deprive you of money is a sign of abuse
- Spending all your money is abuse
- Taking debts in your name is abuse
- Stealing your money is abuse
- Blocking you out of a joint account is abuse
- Travelling and leaving you with no money is abuse
- Seizing you credit and debit card

Emotional Abuse

- Making you feel unworthy
- Telling you if I can't have you no one else will have you. That is possession
- Making you feel dependent
- Extremely apologetic after abuse

Physical Abuse

- Kicking, stalking choking pushing you down the stars, holding you hostage, pulling of hair scourging, pulling shooting with a gun etc shoving slapping throwing object at you
- Asking the kids to beat you. Making dogs bite you. Killing you.
- The more you stay the more it gets worse

Sexual Abuse.

- Rape, making you practice sexual acts against your will is abuse

CHAPTER 5

REASONS WHY VICTIMS STAY

To Protect Their Children

They forget that when you are killed the children will be orphans. You need to be alive to care for your children.

To Preserve the Marriage

Every marriage ends with the death of a party so if you stay and the abuser kills you the marriage is over. You are the single loser. Dead people don't marry. The abuser will remarry and ask God for forgiveness and God will forgive him. So, you better leave and save your life.

What Will People Say?

The dust will settle and you will move on with your life.

I Can Fix This.

You can't fix a monster. They love what they do and derive extreme satisfaction from controlling insulting beating and killing you.

It Is Going to Get Better

I have bad news for you, it is going to get worse. You will soon be in a casket and be a statistic

He Will Never Do It Again

The truth is he will do it again and again and again. He will and you will be in a casket soon if you don't leave.

If Will Love Him More and He Will Change

Only less than 1 percent of abusers change so you will soon be either dead or very sick because of an abuser

Will I Be Happy If I Leave the Abuser?

Yes, you will heal once you leave an abusive partner

It Was a Mistake

If it happened once, you may say it was a mistake even once is unacceptable a man who loves you will never abuse you. When it happens more than once it is a sign that it's not a mistake but deliberate choices made by your abuser to abuse you.

He Apologised.

Forgive him but leave him. An abuser will say anything to keep you in his web of control. His apology is all manipulation.

It Is Gods Will to Flee Abuse and Danger

Recognise that it is not God's will but the will of the devil and to stay in an abusive relationship and suffer illness or be killed. When David realised his life was in danger from Saul he escaped. Jacob fled his manipulative father-in-law and God was still with him.

God warned Laban against harming Jacob in a dream GEN 31.22-24

22 When it was told Laban on the third day that Jacob had fled,

23 he took his kinsmen with him and pursued him for seven days and followed close after him into the hill country of Gilead.

24 But God came to Laban the Aramean in a dream by night and said to him, "Be careful not to say anything to Jacob, either good or bad."

God warned the three wise men not to go back to Herod instead to flee.

When your life is in danger an someone is gradually killing you, it is Gods will to flee

Psalm 103.6 GNT *The Lord judges in favour of the oppressed and gives them their rights*

Bible verse to pray and meditate on Psalm 18:16-20

16 He sent from above, he took me, he drew me out of many waters.

17 He delivered me from my strong enemy, and from them which hated me: for they were too strong for me.

18 They prevented me in the day of my calamity: but the LORD was my stay.

19 He brought me forth also into a large place; he delivered me, because he delighted in me.

20 The LORD rewarded me according to my righteousness; according to the cleanness of my hands hath he recompensed me.

CHAPTER 6

SOLUTIONS

There is a difference between mistakes in a normal relationship and domestic abuse. If you have disagreements with your partner, it's good to seek counselling to repair your relationship. BUT if you are being abused it is best you leave and seek safety. Domestic abuse is deadly don't be a statistic, if you don't feel safe in a relationship or you live in fear, you are walking on eggshells and your partner is verbally and or physically, or financially or emotionally repeatedly abusing you its best you leave. It will be good for you, your children and the abuser.

DOMESTIC VIOLENCE ESCAPE PLAN

1. **A GOOD EXIT PLAN:** Plan your exit carefully; failing to do so may put your life at risk. Act as if everything is okay; do not give any indication that you are planning to leave.

2. **CODED LANGUAGE:** Create a code word to inform loved ones you are in trouble. For example, you might say, "The sky was blue today," "The London marathon," or "Pizza is my favorite food." Don't tell the abuser you want to leave they will either increase the abuse or talk you into staying or panic and kill you or hold you hostage.

3. **CHECK YOUR DEVICES FOR TRACKERS.** Abusers usually track their victim's phone and cars so beware.

4. **Don't believe their flattery**: they will sweet tell you but once you come back you will pay double for attempting to leave. An abuser is like poison the only solution to poison is to leave it. If you keep consuming it will keep hurting you.

5. **DELETE YOUR MESSAGES** Any message you send while planning your escape delete it. Move your important documents little by little to a person you confide with and make photocopies of your important stuff.

6. **CAR keys** If your car keys have been seized you can make a duplicate

7. **CASH** Hide some spare cash to help you reach your save destination

8. **DON'T LEAVE WITHOUT A PLAN. PLANNING IS KEY:** You have to plan where you will go before you leave. E.g. fire station, police station, domestic violence shelter. Or an orphanage Friends and family is not a good idea but if you have strong parents who can stand up to an abuser then its good place beware, he will come there to revenge

9. **DON'T BOW TO PRESSURE FOR A HURRY UNPLANNED EXIT:** Your safety and your children's safety are key. Some zealous friends and family may ask you to leave without careful planning don't do that because it is dangerous. You must plan carefully and leave when it is safe. It is better to stay and endure violence for a few days or weeks or months than to leave hurriedly without planning and trigger a situation that will end your life. Abusers are very dangerous. Many women have been killed because they tried to leave their abusers without planning and leaving at the right time.

10. **LEAVE ONLY WHEN IT IS SAFE:** The most dangerous moment is after you leave. Abusers become extremely dangerous once they realize they are losing control of you. You may need to change your number or block them. They will call 100 times a day, begging,

crying, apologizing, promising it will never happen just to lure you in, then the next time they finish the job you will be dead.

11. **STAY A BIT LONGER IF NECESSARY:** it is better to stay and endure abuse for a few days and carefully plan your escape than to try to leave without a plan
12. **REPORT** Once you report what has happened to you to as many people as possible, silence is the best friend of abusers. They cannot control all people this will put them on the defense and give you some breathing space
13. **LOGOUT** Logout of everything bank accounts social media to make sure your abuser cannot track or trace you.
14. **RECONNECT** Once you leave, reconnect with your trusted friends and family because abusers usually isolate you from friends and family.
15. During this time of need you will see who is for you you can also use the opportunity to cut off all toxic companions. it is an opportunity for a new beginning
16. **Seek counselling** . it is very strange to start a new beginning you may relapse to your abuser if you don't seek counselling
17. Gradually navigate your new life don't rush anything
18. **Throw away** any gifts or letters that connect you to an abuser is like keeping a chain on your neck.
19. **Don't rush** to a new relationship.
20. **GO OFF GRID:** It is essential to disappear for at least one year (DISAPPEAR FROM THE ABUSER) after you leave an abusive relationship because the abuser becomes a mad dog once he finds out you are gone. its best to change your number Change town, stay away from social media, disappear so he doesn't know your location. Domestic violence shelter. Shelter are the best places the police can help you secure shelter or an orphanage or a social welfare center

Things to contemplate if you are experiencing domestic violence

1. A man who beats you up does not love you. You are a mere possession in his eyes or a toy to be used and controlled.
2. A man who loves you will protect and cherish you.

3. Your best way out is if the abuser doesn't know where you are.
4. Your abuser will look for you and try to kill you. Don't Underestimate an abuser.
5. Keep a record of abuse if you can or send it to a confidant. Take photos of injuries or damages and send them to a confidant.
6. Put away money preferably cash for use after exit.
7. Get in touch with a domestic violence advocate groups to help you plan your escape.
8. Identify a family member or friend that you can confide in to help you escape.
9. Leave only when it's safe to leave it better to stay a few days than to leave without a plan and he finds you.
10. Once you leave, tell as many people as possible so that if the abuser shows up, they will tip you off in time to disappear.
11. Go to a place the abusers do not know.
12. Once you leave cut all contact change your sim card and phone number.
13. Identify where you can go and someone will pick you up.
14. Locate your Local domestic violence organisation.
15. Your physical safety is priority.
16. Change your number buy a new sim card if possible.
17. Move to another state or country if possible.
18. Keep a low profile.
19. Don't be online.
20. Get a restraining order but understand that 99 percent of abusers do not respect restraining orders.
21. Make your safety and self-wellbeing a priority.
22. Come to terms with the truth. The person you fell in love with died a long time and you are living with a monster.
23. Build a support system by telling friends and confidants of the abuse.
24. Don't live alone in a house after escaping initially. Because the abuser will come after you.
25. Live with a loved one or in a community because the abuser will seek you when you are alone to kill you.
26. don't let abuser know your location.
27. Avoid isolation situations, be in a community or in public or with people or have a good time and don't be alone.

28. Contact anti domestic violence organisations and seek help to escape and rehabilitate.
29. Contact law enforcement and report your case.
30. Get a restraining order if he is stocking or constantly calling you.
31. Most abusers don't obey restraining orders so run for your life. A man who stalks you will kill you when he gets the chance.
32. Live in a community and avoid isolation.
33. Cut contacts because the abuser will lure you into his web if you maintain communication.
34. Done be alone don't be alone don't be alone.
35. The abuser seeks your isolation. Let loved ones take turns to keep you company.
36. Invest in camera technology around your house if you can afford it.
37. Abusers always come a lie in waiting for you to come home.

CHAPTER 7

SOCIETAL RESPONSIBILITY

Responsibility Of Friends and Relatives

1. Talk to victims about what you think and the dangers of denial
2. Constantly check on loved ones. Don't assume all is well
3. Visit loved ones an seek private opportunities to talk to loved ones
4. Contact law enforcement on behalf of loved ones
5. Calmly talk to victims and offer your help and support
6. Don't judge victims

Responsibility Of the Public

1. If you see something wrong say something
2. Call the police when you hear neighbours fighting
3. Don't be indifferent
4. Advocate for longer sentences for offenders
5. Stalking must be severely punished
6. Advocate for ankle bracelets to be imposed on abuser who stalk victims

Responsibility Of Governments

1. Increase funding of domestic violence agencies
2. Government needs to create more shelters for victims of violence
3. They have to Create special agencies to focus on the issue of domestic violence
4. Train police be able to respond properly
5. Government must create red flag laws that stops abusers from accessing weapons
6. Restraining orders must be enforced with ankle bracelets
7. Create hotline numbers so victims can seek help
8. Train agents to answer distress calls and provide help
9. Governments should consider using ankle trackers to enforce restraining order on abusers

Warnings

1. The first 1 year after break up is the most dangerous. Your ex may be plotting your execution take precautions.
2. If you leave an abuser and live alone in an apartment, he is coming to kill you
3. Change your locks buy a dog
4. Don't live alone. Have a community around you.
5. Isolation is the abuser's best tool. Don't give him that.
6. Avoid accepting a ride from people you don't know it may be death trap.

Help Centres You Can Call and Get Help

1. Contact the police
2. Google domestic violence advocates and establish contact.
3. Local orphanages can offer you temporary shelter
4. Please contact your local domestic violence centre
5. If there is none, contact social homes
6. The police; fire station, or orphanage desperate situations require desperate measures
7. If you are in USA
8. Call the US National domestic violence Hotline at 18007997233
9. Please contact local agencies of your country for help.
10. Women's law .org.
11. Domestic violence women's advocacy service

Beware Of Liars

Some people lie about being abused to attract public sympathy or to assassinate the characters of others and to get fame. Make sure you investigate allegations thoroughly before you Conclude.

How To Locate Liars.

They are more interested in contacting the media than anti abuse organisations to get help them rehabilitate.

Crying Call

Let's put our hands together and defeat domestic violence.

About The Author

The author Bebuh Divine is an Evangelist with a burning love for Christ. He is also an activist working to end the pandemic of domestic violence. He believes all people must be treated with dignity and respect regardless of race, religion, gender, income, social status etc

All interest in distributing this book contact the author at

divinebebuh22@gmail.com

www.ingramcontent.com/pod-product-compliance
Lightning Source LLC
Chambersburg PA
CBHW040809150726
48196CB00058B/1467